CORE VALUE THERAPY

DAVID NANCARROW

ISBN-13: 978-0-9757858-1-2

I wish to first dedicate this book to the wonderful counsellor: Isaiah 9:6.

CONTENTS

FOREWORD

It has been some time since we have seen an effective technique developed and evolve in such a way that is easily explained to clients and easily understood by clients. The experiential nature of Core Value Therapy (CVT) provides a real-time grounding for those who have accurately identified their core value through CVT and experience this grounding as a comfort. No longer is it an unpleasant, unsettling set of emotions but an awareness of one's own aroused core value. Arousal is progressively reduced as the use of CVT principals are adopted. Extinction of arousal is also possible with intentional application. CVT has an easy to understand rationale and is truly a technique that can stand alone, beside or integrated into any therapist's existing models or practice. Your clients will thank you. Thank you David for this wonderful gift. — Trevor Reeve (Manager No 34 Aboriginal Health)

PREFACE

A journey as a counsellor is an interesting one. You help people through life's problems and observe a personal growth in yourself. Every now and then a client significantly changes your world view and it was on one of these occasion in 2007 when I meet a male client who changed my life.

The session was for anger management and started out like any other session. However, my frustration of not really being able to significantly address the real issue regarding anger was starting to build up. Strategies I applied were about assisting the client to calm down after being angry and looking at the triggers that roused their anger in the first place. But what if we could look at the real cause and where was this to be found?

The client said, 'people press his button'. I had had enough; I had heard what seemed to me a thousand other clients saying the same thing over the last few weeks. I launched out of my chair and drew a button circle shape on the white board and said, 'we are not going to leave this room until we find what is this button!'

I look back on that day and think it felt like I stumbled across what has now become known as 'Core Value Therapy' (CVT). All I know is that I am truly grateful and amazed of how many lives this therapy has changed. Other therapists are embracing CVT into their practise as a core part of most other therapies they apply.

Could this be a new yet complementing therapeutic approach as we haven't had a new therapy for over 40 years? I let you be the judge.

Many who have been trained in CVT across Australia have said it is one thing to learn CVT, another to deliver it and yet the most significant part is to personally experience it.

May I conclude with my humble appreciation of the clients CVT has helped not only control their emotions but improve their understanding of themselves and their relationships around them.

Many have found their button and turn it off.

INTRODUCTION

Core Value Introduction

Core value therapy started with a client of mine in early 2007. The client came for anger management and kept mentioning people kept pressing their button. I made a circle on the white board and said, 'we are going to find this button'. This began a conversation about what bothered them about other people's actions towards them. What was revealed was a **value word.**

I observed in clients that their particular value was influencing their anger. For example, clients would say, *'I don't like it when other people disrespect me and don't accept what I have to say.'* This may not sound like some amazing revelation, as we can all relate to hearing clients say these sorts of things. The critical discovery I have made with statements like this, is clients do not actually hear the majority of these value words. For example, in the above statement, the value words 'respect' and 'acceptance'. Assisting clients to discover, connect with and take charge of their value words is now known as 'Core Value Therapy'.

Core Value Therapy assists the client to have greater awareness of self by allowing them to see what influences their behaviours, emotions and cognitive functions. Greater awareness significantly improves a client's locus of control. Although circumstances may trigger a response in a client, their changing nature cannot be truly relied upon to assist them to find true answers towards change. It is their unique values which remain constant in their lives and guide them to a changed response. Once a client can observe that their values are the source of their emotions they develop an even greater self-awareness. This increased self-awareness greatly improves the client's ability for self-control. When a client knows their core value they are not as aroused emotionally when things do not go as they have planned, or when their values have been breached. Clients also show an ability to discuss past emotional interactions with people that has caused significant distress, with a greater sense of calmness, this is incredible to observe. For the client they are amazed and their self-awareness allows them to do this. Their confidence lifts tremendously and they see that change is possible for them. The strength for this change comes from greater awareness of their personal values. The results are ongoing and lasting.

When a client understands that others can't fulfil their core value but they must fulfil it for themselves first, their core value becomes healthier it can now be given as a gift to others. Emotional regulation and behaviour improves remarkably in the client, which in turn positively lifts the client's self-esteem and relationships with others.

Key aspects of Core Value Therapy

One key aspect of Core Value Therapy is listening for value words in stories which have made clients feel strong feelings – mainly feelings such as anger, becoming annoyed or offended. These stories are embedded with values. These values influence a client's behaviour, thoughts and emotions.

Once a client discovers their core value they improve remarkably well in their emotional regulation when applying the core value to themselves in situations distressing to them. It is very much like the core value is the centre of the problem and then becomes the answer to that problem. In this way it tends to shift the 'locus of control' from the other person back to themselves.

Another key aspect of Core Value Therapy is the acknowledgement that clients do not hear themselves say their core value words despite saying them very frequently. Clients' core values are hidden from their conscious mind. Therefore, they are operating from an unconscious state. Many clients have told me they do not know why they get angry and can't make sense of it. The moment the value is revealed it makes sense to them what is going on and they begin to see the world completely differently, through a different lens.

When clients apply their value correctly to themselves and to others, they report increase in self-esteem, improvement in relationships and stabilisation of emotion regulation. This approach is explained in more detail in the 'Clinician Techniques for Core Value Therapy' section.

For most practitioners, when we hear the clients' stories on a daily basis, we get engrossed in the circumstances and details of that story, want to know what is going on, focus on their feelings and focus on solutions. All this is good and worthwhile while we often miss the main point. The main point is found in what types of value words the client uses to tell their story. It represents the meaning of the story to them. Over ten years practising Core Value Therapy, I have observed clients use countless different value words. I do not interpret that value word, change it or put my own spin on it.

Most practitioners who attend Core Value Therapy training state they have to learn to listen differently to their clients from now on and will need to expand their vocabulary on what constitutes a 'core value word'. This is because the value words each client uses are sometimes unique and always most definitely important to them. It is not too difficult to hear the value words in everyday speech or in a problem once you know how. The key is buying into this particular word being the driving force for that person, and as stated previously, is the main influence for their thoughts, behaviours and emotional reactions. You as the practitioner will be the catalyst to assist the client in discovering, hearing and applying their personal value words correctly in their lives.

A third key aspect of Core Value Therapy is not to reveal the values to the client. They need to hear their own value themselves. If you tell the client their value word they will not believe you and it can devalue the moment. Please refer to the 'Therapeutic Method' section where the therapy approach is explained in more detail on how to assist the client in finding their core value.

OVERVIEW

In brief the Core Value model is:

- **Listen to the client tell a story that has upset them in some way.** This can be a rather long story – let this happen without interrupting them.
- **Note the value words they use.** It can be quite difficult to not get caught up in the story by asking inquiring questions and starting to talk about their feelings. It does become easier with time and it is like you hear a different dialogue containing the value words.
- **Get them to repeat the story.** The story will become shorter and shorter until you have a sentence. You are doing this to see for yourself if any of the value words start to repeat themselves.

- **Note these values.**

If the value words start repeat you can relax a bit because, this is the beginning of identifying the core ones. There are 'sub values' and 'core values' and this is explained in the following 'Therapeutic Method' section in more detail. Even a sub value which is causing some emotional reaction in the client is good for the client to know.

Once the client repeats a particular value (in their shorten story) point this out to the client, 'you just mentioned a value word can you recall it?' (While this does slightly interrupts the client to reflect back on what they just said, this needs to occur).

Most clients cannot recall what they have just said. (Discovering their core value improves a client's ability to recall what they have spoken.) They will to go over the sentence and the spot of the value word will appears blank to them. They might replace that value word with another word from their conscious mind but you must not go with this. You want them to recall the original value word.

Proceed with the story or if the last repeated statement has the original value word in it get the client to write it down or get them to repeat it back, further still seek their permission to record it on their or your phone and then play it back to them. Replay the recording back to them as it is often the case the client still cannot hear themselves say the value word.

It gets very exciting once the value word is there in front of them.

Do not reveal the value word to them no matter how tempting this may be.

At this stage the client will usually say, 'D*id I say <value word>?'* I repeat every time back to them, *'I don't know, did you say <pause>...'* (But I don't say the word even now). I deliberately doubt them. Why? Because they need to discover if for themselves, they respect and value it more. If you do affirm it, the unconscious mind does not communicate with the conscious mind.

This communication is a very important process; it needs to occur and is a vital step in Core Value Therapy. The client will often pause and think; allow this to go on for a little while. Do not interrupt them during time of reflection as they are going over past events in their mind. They will often say, *'Oh! I say <value word>? All the time!'* This does not devalue the whole therapy approach at this point, no this confirms it. Why? What has just occurred is the client has now seen for the first time their past experiences through the lens of the core value word. Some even go as far back as their childhood.

What occurs next is fascinating – they often laugh and brighten up. Whereas a few moments ago they were distressed talking about their problem, struggling with it wrestling with it. What is also wonderful to observe is the client can talk about the original problem with much greater emotional regulation thereafter.

I am sure we all know clients who can talk about their problem session after session with often growing emotional turmoil. What occurs in clients who have discovered their core value is they are able to make sense of many aspects of their life that has troubled them. Understand why they were hurt, angry or upset.

From there I take them through the three areas of how the core value influences their life. From others, to others, and to themselves. For further explanation on this please refer to the 'Clinician's Technique for Core Value Therapy' section.

Core Value Therapy appears to work well with practitioners who have some underpinning counselling methodology influencing their practise such as Narrative therapy, Cognitive Behavioural Therapy, Response Therapy, Solution Focus and Acceptance Commitment Therapy. All these can be used in conjunction with Core Value Therapy.

CORE VALUE THERAPY

What is Core Value Therapy?

In Core Value Therapy (CVT) the practitioner works with the client to discover their core value (CV). In nearly all cases, the client is unaware of their CV and yet it is central to their thoughts, feelings, behaviours and bodily state.

Once the CV has been unlocked and identified, the client can experience a greater understanding of how their CV effects their interactions with others and themselves. This awareness can lead to a healthier respect for their CV and their expectations of others and themselves meeting their CV. Through this understanding, a person's internal locus of control is strengthened and an improved emotional regulation is observed.

The goal of CVT is to empower the client to respond to

life from a place where the Primary Core Value (PCV) is a healthy not reacting to others not meeting their PCV needs.

What type of clients is CVT effective for?

CVT has application in the areas of anger management, conflict resolution and personal and relationship counselling.

What is a value?

In essence a value is whatever brings value to the client. There are different types of values: primary core values, sub-core values and other values that may be important to the individual.

PRIMARY CORE VALUE

What is a Primary Core Value?

Through work in this field for over ten years, experience has demonstrated that everyone has a 'Primary Core Value' (PCV) that dominates their behaviour, thinking and emotional regulation. The PCV filters everything in the person's life; nothing escapes it. The PCV is very personal. The person may state it in the negative: e.g. I felt unappreciated, disrespected, no one understands me, they are incapable, or incompetent.

It appears that this PCV cannot be changed. It has been part of an individual's life since early childhood when clients reflect on their PCV in operation from a very young age.

The PCV may not be one of the common value words such as respect, honesty, integrity, trust or approval. The therapist must broaden their definition of a value to be able to recognise it in their client. These may include value words such as, that is not <u>right</u>, what is the <u>point</u>, that is not good <u>enough</u> and that's <u>important</u>.

When an individual feels angry, wounded or offended they experience a rush of emotions or negative thoughts are activated by their PCV which in turn influence their behaviour.

How is the PCV established? Are we born with a PCV (NATURE) or does it develop at a very young age (NURTURE)? I consider both are relevant. In any case I have observed in clients that when client un lock their Primary Core value they have memories of this value being breach at a very young age. I could be reasonable to say it is form in the formative years of life.

SUB-CORE VALUES

What are sub-Core Values?

Sub-Core Values (SCVs) or Sub Values are a cluster of about three values that dominate their life. Some people have more but it is usually three. These sub-values are used as required in different situations, whereas the PCV is present in every situation.

Other important values

Individuals may also hold other socially accepted values that have been instilled in them by society, their company they work for, families, religion or from education. These may be congruent with their SCVs or even their PCV. It is important to acknowledge the role that these values play in their life. When values are in opposition to their PCV or SCVs the individual can experience conflict within themselves and in relationships.

THERAPEUTIC METHOD

Therapeutic method – Stage 1

Unlocking the client PCV through an experiential process

Unlocking the PCV (steps for therapist)

1. Begin with establishing rapport and explain briefly that during the session you will be assisting the client to become aware of their core value.
2. Invite the client to describe a situation which evoked an emotional response. Let the client tell the story relatively uninterrupted.
3. Whilst the client is speaking, listen for the value words, note the client's repetition of a particular words. It is the meaningful words in the story that

you are locating. Usually the clinician can hear the CV consistently throughout their dialogue. Note these words down.

4. It is important the clinician does not encourage the client to get caught up in the circumstances or feelings. The main aim of CVT is to highlight the value words used. The therapist aims to amplify the client's responses by asking enquiring questions, such as why did that situation bother you?

5. Be prepared to have a broad range of what defines a value word. In essence it is whatever brings value to the client. Therefore, if you eliminate the circumstances and somewhat the feelings from the story then what is left is the value word which highlights all what the client is feeling and explains why the circumstances are affecting then so much.

6. Once the clinician is fairly sure of the PCV, ask the client to repeat the story. It will be naturally shorter and more focussed even down to a sentence. It is very reassuring for the clinician to hear the values words from the client being repeated.

7. Repetitively doing this, when the values are embedded in the story, allows the clinician to make mention of the occurrence to the client, 'I

heard you mention some value words when you were telling me the story about your life, do you recall them?'

8. The story can come down to one sentence or even a short phraze and the values will be there.

9. Recording the client and playing back the sentence containing their PCV is very powerful. Especially when they cannot hear it. Even asking the client to write down the sentence and underline the values they see. Use the question 'did you hear yourself use a value word?'

10. At first the client is fixed on the specific circumstances which lead to them experiencing the heightened emotions, and so cannot reflect and hear their own reactions. The individual can sometimes experience their PCV in their body, but are not aware of bodily reactions. This may be another line of enquiry.

11. They may see some sub core value (SCV) but often miss the very value that is in the PCV. The therapist validating the SCVs and reinforcing their importance in various life circumstances can build momentum for the client to discover their PCV, which applies to every aspect of their life..

12. When clients discover their PCV they all show an emotional reaction, although their individual emotional response can be unique. Clients often

concluded the discovery process with smiles a relief and joy.

13. Resist all temptation to tell the client the value word. For it to be meaningful and powerful, they need to discover it themselves. If the therapist points out the PCV there is the risk of devaluating the session, as the client may not believe it or accept it. It has to be an "Ah-ha" moment for the client. Honour this moment of revelation.

14. The therapist must be able to sit comfortably with the client's uncertainty while they contemplate and come to terms with the PCV now revealed to them.

15. With the PCV identified, it needs to be tested. Does it fit a situation in childhood? A situation as a teenager? In the present? If not, it is probably a SCV.

16. Go back over the stories that the client has shared at the beginning of the session. Apply the value back into those stories . This allows the client to observe the story from a different perspective and greater understanding.

UNLOCKING THE PRIMARY CORE VALUE

The 'BULLS EYE' method for unlocking the PCV

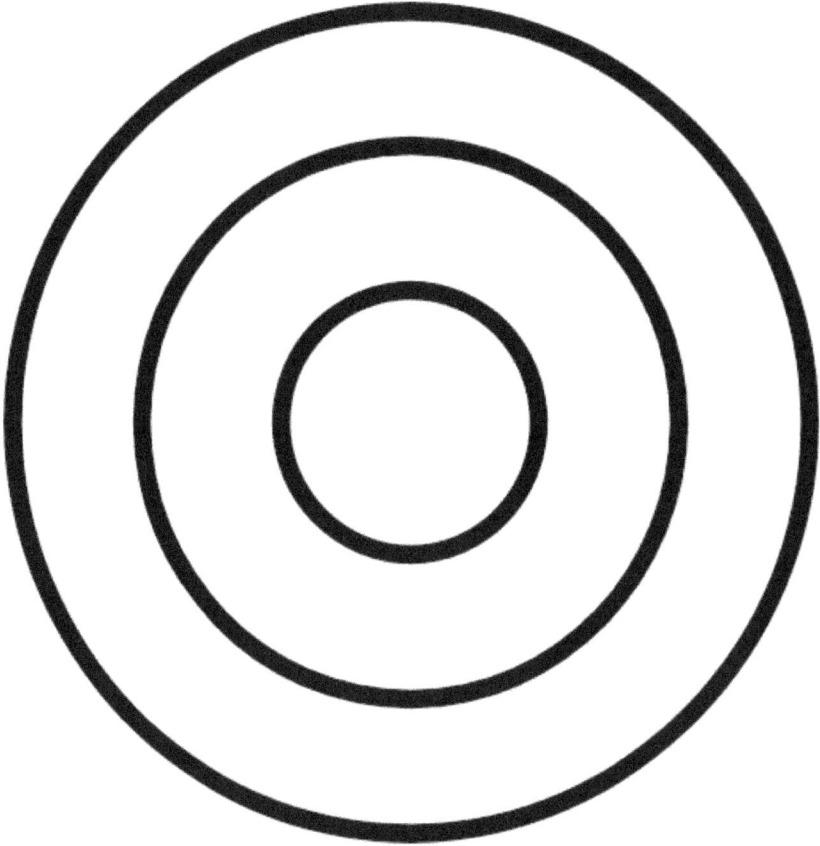

1. Start with writing the summary of their problem situation on the outer ring of the target, for example:

2. *I came home from work; I had a crap day and had a lot on my mind. As soon as I walked in the door she was at me.*

3. Proceed to ask questions such as *'Why does that bother you?'*

4. Write the answer down. It is important to write down the exact answer using the clients' words, for example you may hear:

5. *'I am angry because....... people are so rude'*

6. *'I get depressed when....... someone doesn't respect my things'*

7. *'I get stressed when......people do not appreciate what I do.'*

8. It is surprising to see client's reactions when they see what they said.

9. Disallow the client to reword an answer or fall back to, "I don't know it just makes me angry."

10. Notice when the statements shift to reveal more personal behaviours.

11. *'They didn't want to listen to me'*

12. *'I get frustrated and just want to be left alone'*

13. *'I really don't care anymore'*

14. *'They don't feel heard! Well I sure don't feel heard'*

15. *'I feel trapped'*

16. *'I don't like being blamed for things I didn't do'*

17. Keep asking until you get to the centre, for example by using their last answer as the starting point for your next question until the 'value' emerges:

18. C: *"They didn't want to listen to me"* – T: *"What is the reason someone not listening to you makes you*

*angry?" - C:"I don't feel heard" – T: "What upsets you about not being heard?" C: "It's not **fair;** I listen to them, so they should listen to me."*

GENERAL DISCUSSION

Discussion:

It is a real skill to listen to the client's story whilst also picking up on value words, which are the lens through which the client evaluates their experience with the world.

While circumstances and stories change, the primary core value is consistent in every situation. If the client uses different value words for different situations, then any value words used are probably a sub-core value. When you hear the client use the same value word as they tell you about different situations which caused them to be upset, you can with great certainty know that you have probably struck their PVC.

The clients generally cannot hear themselves use their value words. In the past fourteen years of applying Core Value Therapy, this observation has remained constant. Just prior to a client's realisation about a value, they doubt if the value word they have been using is the right one. If the clinician pauses in this moment, allowing the client to reflect without being interrupted, the full revelation can occur. Some relate it to a light bulb moment.

Many clients, but not everyone, recall several past experiences which connect with their core value and start to make meaning of those experiences. Some clients even go as far back as their childhood, usually when the value was not met or breached by others. This supports Erickson's theory of generativity when values are broken in early childhood development.

THERAPEUTIC METHOD – STAGE 2

Gaining awareness of PCV operating in relationship with self and others

PCV – good use and bad use

- The next step is to explore their PCV – What does it look like? What does it feel like when it's operating well, or operating poorly?
- Using the example through which they discovered their PCV, ask *'Why did you behave in a particular way? Did you enjoy your response? What were the real reasons behind your response?"*
- Keep pressing the client gently but firmly.

During this stage it is important that the client does not

feel judged, and does not fixate on blame towards themselves or others.

Often the client will highlight how disappointed they were during times of others not meeting their PCV and in response behaved directly opposite to their PCV towards the offender.

Example: In a case where the client's PCV is trust, and as others have let them down, they behave in an untrustworthy way towards others and themselves.

PCV – From others, to others and towards self

The therapist can explore when the PCV has worked for the client and when it has been breached. This can be a good opportunity to explore the good aspect of the clients values. When it has been met by other, when they have given it away positively. When conflict occurs, it often relates to the high expectations they place on themselves and on others meeting their CV. In particular, the following applications:

- Receiving the CV from others
- Giving the CV to others
- Giving the CV to themselves (the client).

FROM OTHER - TO OTHERS - TO THEMSELVES

From others:

- Clients want their PCV met by others and when it is not, conflict results within the client and within relationships around them.
- When clients are asked how much out of ten they want others to meet their PCV, all clients indicate 8, 9 even 10 out of 10.
- The clinician needs to point out the difficult task for others to meet this standard –Expect the client to resist, as they believe their sense of value is maintained by having this high standard.
- At this stage the client may start to develop an awareness of their unrealistic expectations and

how this may lead to tension and conflict with others.

- If the client sets the bar too high they will always be disappointed.
- Present to the client what would occur to lower your expectation of others meeting you Core Value.
- Clients will consider that if they lower it they will devalue themselves. However the opposite occurs, they increase in value and are not as emotional when others do not meet their values and at he same time maintain their values. If they don't consider this aspect of CVT the client will breach their value in order to make others maintain it back to them!
- It can also be observed that others may not share the person's PCV and therefore it is hard for them to provide it to the person in the form they expect.

To others:

- The clinician then asks the client how much they behave in a way that is consistent with their PCV towards others.
- Gently highlight the client's part in breaching their CV in their relationships with others. With the increased knowledge and awareness of their CV,

draw out the fact that they (the client) has breached the very same value they have judged others for failing to meet. This is a very important point.

- At this stage there are not many clients that can resist this evidence, and conviction comes. With over 1000 clients who have gone through the CVT since 2007, 99% have embraced this change in their story. The change being, instead of talking about the external story they are now reflecting and talking about their responses to others.

- Previously clients may have justified their actions, saying others deserved them acting in a certain way. The client in the past may have seen no correlation with their actions being a breach of the very same value they were so upset about breaching with them. The reason for this is that up until this point the client has been unaware of their CV and therefore had limited awareness and knowledge of their own breach of this value.

To themselves

- The therapist can also ask the client how much they give their core value to themselves. Most of the time they will respond 2 or 3/10.
- The reason this is so low is due to people often

'crossing the line' or 'over retaliating' when others breach their value toward them. It is their hot button, and a hot response is triggered. As a result, they feel horrible and score their value to themselves very low.

- For example, someone breaches the client's value of respect. The client feels angry to a point of expressing their anger in a manner that is disrespectful towards the offender. They then did not respect themselves. This is explained further in the following:

The client breaches their own values to themselves and to others

- Following the discovery of their CV it is important to reveal to the client they have breached their own values. This can and usually occurs in the same session. This may appear too much, but the window of opportunity is open and it is the best time to complete the next part of the CVT journey.
- To do this, go back over the original story. Within that story there will be evidence that the client has indeed breached his or her own CV. This needs to be gently pointed out to them. It is

holding up a mirror, allowing the client to reflect on their behaviour and not on that of others.

- Clients display an unusual acceptance of the fact that they have breached their own value. This self-reflection brings about real conviction and change in the client.

- Through open discussion with the clinician the client accepts their part in breaching their values to others. They see that breaching their values back to others was indeed within their control and responsibility. It is wonderful to observe clients showing genuine change in their behaviour and the ability to emotionally regulate themselves in the stories they share in subsequent counselling sessions.

Discussion:

Following the three Core Value directions, from others, to others to self previouly outlined, now discussion with the client can centre on what the client can control and what they can't control. If their self-efficacy comes from others they may be disappointed as they can't control how others behave towards them, and others don't know what they need nor understand their PCV. It is like being on an emotional roller coaster from tears, laughter, increased awareness through the journey of discovering the clients cove value.

A person's relationship with their PCV

Unhealthy feedback spiral

Expect from others feel disappointed become angry with others behave opposite to PCV Self-hate, feel unworthy of their PCV.

Healthy feedback

Understand PCV Give to self feel congruent with inner CV give to others get back from others or may not (not dependent on this).

THERAPEUTIC METHOD - STAGE 3

Doing nothing but simply observing the PCV

It is a relief for a client to identify their primary core value however; some clients are very concerned about what to do about it. It can be very overwhelming. They have just had a major discovery about how they think, act and make decisions according to their primary core value and now the CVT model wants them to do nothing about it!

I admit, this does sound rather strange, but this is an important part of the CVT model. The client needs to relax and be given permission by the counsellor to do nothing about it. This allows the client to observe the primary core value at work. They need to see why they react differently. The primary core value will keep on working for better or worse and they need to observe both responses, good and bad. In doing this they can objectively test the primary core value and ask *'Does it really affect all parts of my life?'*

Therapeutic method - Stage 3

Accepting the PCV

The client needs to accept the primary core value as the issue that affects and influences their situation. If the client is in any doubt, then the value discovered may be a sub-value. In this case:

- Take them through the core value exercise again and fine tune it to reveal the primary core value.
- Once a new primary core value is identified then the client is encouraged to repeat Stage 3 and observe it over the next week or so.
- Clients need to observe their reactions during real-life experiences with the primary core value on their mind.

It is always important to remind them the primary core value is usually hidden to them. It is in their subconscious, yet at the same time in their speech and the very thing that they live by. It can be a strange dichotomy for a counsellor to witness this. The moment a client recognises it is not circumstances or other people that are the reason for their anger being triggered, but their primary core value at the centre of all – they get it!

Blaming begins to stop and acceptance of their own reactions begins.

Therapeutic method Stage 4

Apply and adjust the Primary Core Value

This stage of adjusting the PCV in the client is very important in CVT. In all clients, their expectations of others fulfilling their core value is set too high, which makes it an target for others to maintain.

- Draw a scale on the whiteboard 0-10 and then ask *'How high would you like your <primary core value> be fulfilled by others?'* All clients state around 8 or 9, out of 10.
- Reply that this is very difficult for others to achieve. They have to get a near perfect score in fulfilling your primary core value for you to accept it as good enough.

I have some clients who knew they were a perfectionist and their answers to the above question were 11 out of 10! This is, of course, impossible for others to fulfil. They agreed, 'it is never good enough'. This is an important point for clients who score eight our ten it is often never good enough. Most people need it to be set high for them to feel respected, appreciated, accepted or valued in some way. However, if others do not match the level set and only offer a lesser amount, let's say 5 or 6 out of 10, then that's when offence, hurt and emotions are experienced. It sets up people in the client's life to fail.

What can a client do? To keep up the standard will not work, as clients are really saying continually in their mind and heart others shall respect, accept or honour me.

Discussion:

A client's primary core value is like their radar constantly scanning their surroundings. Clients will notice it not being fulfilled by others or themselves and it presses their primary core value button. Things become untenable when a client is driven to think the world needs to satisfy their core value. They are like a dry sponge needing others to fulfil their primary core value and fill them up.

- At this stage of the session, encourage the person to lower the standard from 9 to below five, ideally as low as 2 out of 10. This is an interesting concept for most people to grasp when they have spent most of their life holding up their standard and expecting others to respect them; honour them, and validate them whatever their primary core may be.
- One thing you have in your favour when people

struggle with this concept of lowering their core value standard is their past. You can mention to clients they may choose to do nothing and the one thing which will most likely occur is that nothing will change. A client's past is evidence of this and continues to get the same results as before.

Most ask how they lower the standard they are expecting from others. I say, 'instead of asking how do you lower this, ask yourself why are you holding it up this high?' *When a clients core value is breached by others the metre of wanting this value to be met by others goes up. Over time it reaches the point of being too high for people to actually met that standard.* reinforcing to the client that others are letting them down and the value does not work. it becomes their enemy rather than their best friend.

Further more helping clients lower their core value standard can be achieved by asking, *'Another way to explain this is to ask yourself have you ever forgiven someone?'* Everyone I have asked this has responded in the affirmative. I asked them *'How did you do this, how do you explain what happen?'* I sum it up simply as in letting it go and not holding on to it anymore.

Likewise, if the client can let go of their expectation of others needing to fulfil their core value, I find it will rest at about 2 out of 10 for them.

Apply the primary core value to the client.

- Introduce a second meter on the whiteboard. This meter represents them the same scale of 0-10.
- Ask, *'Out of 10, how much do you fulfil your own primary core value to yourself?'* Most clients will indicate they find it difficult to apply their core value to themselves – to accept or respect themselves.
- If clients have high expectations of others to fulfil their core value, then they have an equally low level of self-acceptance to themselves. This is usually a very confronting moment for clients as they want others to accept, acknowledge and respect them but they cannot do it to themselves. There is a direct correlation to the client's high expectation from others and their low application of their value to themselves. They are asking others to do what they can not do for themselves.
- Reflect back to the client that we can't control the responses from other. We can only control our responses. Draw this on the while board or on paper to make it visual to them.

Therapeutic method Stage 6

Understanding and using the PCV as a gift to give yourself and others:

This is really about moving from victim or aggressor, to a positive engagement with themselves and the world. Using this primary core value as a gift to others is a wonderful stage to introduce to clients.

- Introduce the concept that their core value is a 'GIFT'. It is not meant to be satisfied by others to the client, it is meant to be given to others by the client. For example, one might want respect but needs to consider giving respect to others.
- Some, not all, clients doubt this concept because their worldview, like most of us, is centred on ourselves. Clients can still say *'but I like people respecting me, accepting, and acknowledging me.'* All this can seem good on the surface but
- Remind them what happens when others don't acknowledge them enough according to their metre out of 10. Remind them that in the past they used to get angry and offended when this didn't work. Their behaviour is unlikely to improve if they continue in this way.
- Offer them the choice between continuing to react to situations which offend them or consider they have something (their CV) to offer others which can greatly assist the situation will help them in return.
- Point out, by using their primary core value as a

gift, it can help rather than harm others and also help rather than harm themselves. When a person is unable to meet their own core values they can experience anxiety, stress, regret and depression.

- Guide the client to the understanding, their core value needs to be a person's own best friend, not their enemy. For them to take control of their life, they must realise the core value is the solution not the problem. If they operate poorly in their core value this not only hurts others be will hurt themselves.

Role of therapist

To be able to use CVT, the therapist is expected to know his or her own CV. Like any therapeutic model if you use it in your own life it becomes more authentic to your clients. To know your own CV requires a trained clinician to work with the therapist through the process as described above.

Interactions with others therapies

CVT is compatible with other therapy models. Awareness of their values can shift a client's perception; unlocking a piece of a person's puzzle, a core part of their being. Therapy models such as Cognitive Behavioural Therapy (CBT), Mindfulness, Acceptance and Commitment Therapy (ACT) and Schema Therapy can then support the person in their awareness and changing old patterns of thought and behaviour with the new awareness. CBT, for example, can enlighten how the CVT drives thoughts, emotions and behaviour.

Model for envisaging the role of the CVT and CBT.

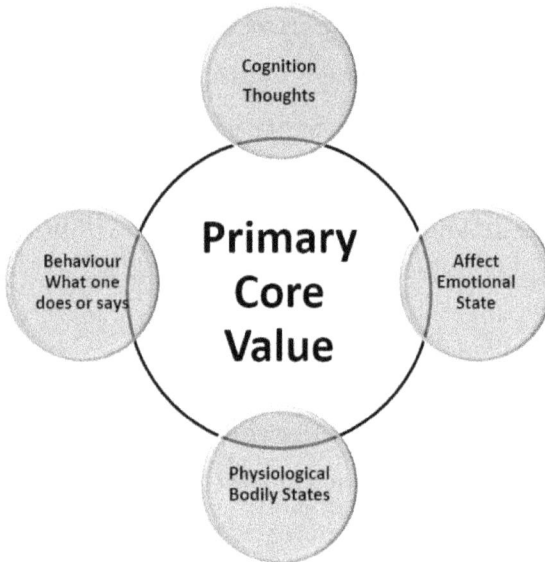

Core Value therapy considers the CV influences feeling, cognitive functions and behaviours.

Cognitive Behavioural Therapy (CBT) encourages the client to understand how their negative thoughts influence their behaviour. These negative thoughts are underpinned by dysfunctional rules and these in turn by core beliefs, which are fundamental and often unconscious beliefs about self, others and the world. It is at this level where Core Value Therapy digs yet deeper again, assisting with uncovering the key and core value of the individual. This core value surpasses all other beliefs, thoughts and emotions.

Due to this clients demonstrate greater emotional regulation and higher cognitive functioning once they have become aware of their core values.

This can be observed when the client goes through a thought process using their prefrontal cortex to lower their expectation of their value from others and deciding to give their value away to others. Previously, clients demonstrated a continuous lack of emotional regulation when their values were breached, incapable of any logical or rational thought. The higher functional part of their brain was previously controlled by their amygdala and limbic system, which responded in "flight" behaviours such as flight, for example verbally "*I don't have to put up with this I am of here*' or expressed in non-verbal behaviour such as withdrawal. They may also respond with 'fight' behaviours such as verbal aggression or 'freeze' behaviour, such as not being able to say or do anything. When a client has become aware, that is brought the core value from the unconscious into the conscious, they can look back at these past events in their life and know why they responded in the way they did and gain insight.

Over the last 10 years of using Core Value Therapy,

clients have been observed to display greater control over their emotions when encountering ongoing relationship conflict, which is extremely encouraging. Often their improved reactions to these conflicts have greatly enhanced their relationships for the better.

THERAPIST VIEW OF CORE VALUE THERAPY — DR SABRINA MARTIN PHD (CLINICAL PSYCHOLOGIST)

I have been using Core Value Therapy (CVT) for a while now. The biggest impact I have seen in clients is that the model can directly shift a person's locus of control back to themselves. After being caught up in the externalised version of their story, and being emotionally activated by this, it brings the focus back onto themselves and brings the capacity to self-regulate. Because the core value is inherently personal to the client, they deeply connect with it. This is why it is then easily generalised beyond the initial problem discussed in session to other circumstances and other areas of their life.

It is clearly a model in its own right, but compatible for use with other therapy models (e.g. ACT, CBT, Schema Therapy etc). Like other therapy models, it is essential to learn it experientially. To be able to apply the model the therapist has to experience the impact that discovering ones own value has and how we can be completely blind to it before it is revealed. The shift away from getting upset about how others breach the value to us and instead becoming aware of how and when we breach the value to ourselves and others has a significantly empowering effect.

When first learning to apply the model in therapy, the hardest learning curve was learning to listen to the client's story (their thoughts, their feelings and patterns of reacting) but in parallel also hearing their value words and distinguishing between some more superficial values and the core one. Although it still has some benefit with a subvalue, best results are achieved with the core value, which are linked to a deeper emotional and physiological response.

Dr Sabrina Martin (PhD Clin Psychology), MAPS (Clin College)

THERAPIST VIEW OF CORE VALUE THERAPY — SINÉAD FAHEY, PSYCHOLOGIST

I was trained in Core Value Therapy (CVT) in 2016 and have used it in my practice with clients. I appreciate that CVT is a stand-alone process that also successfully stands beside modalities such as schema and cognitive behaviour therapy. In my practice I have particularly focussed on its suitability for integration with somatically focussed processes and find that it links successfully.

In my observations, the process of CVT has a remarkably powerful effect for a person as they experience the 'bringing forward' of their core value from the unconscious to conscious mind. As the person connects with their core value it integrates with memories and everyday interactions that might ordinarily have been puzzling or invited a distress/high volume response. I have observed with clients, that as connection with the core value occurs, dysregulation is more easily identified and self-regulation would appear to be more automatic. It is almost as though an insight barrier is removed and opens opportunities to understand how to initiate a new interaction with self and the world around them.

People that have worked through the process have reported a different way of understanding their situation, have noticed that they can follow through on goals and activities that might have otherwise been challenging for them and initiated new ways of communicating in relationships. I have found the investigation of how the value is applied to self, to others and from others to be very advantageous in supporting the person to understand themselves and the changes in their lives that would better support the life they would like to live.

Utilising the therapy in practice is an ongoing skill development in terms of filtering out core and sub values and in developing the listening skills to do so. The clinician needs to maintain confidence and trust in the process during the often clunky leap for the client from unconscious to conscious awareness. I believe it is essential to have experienced the process personally (which is not intrusive) to gain some insight into what you are walking the client through, to help you believe in the process and of course to understand the gains you can make from identifying you own unique and individual core value!

. . .

Sinéad Fahey, Psychologist Dec - 2018

A STUDENT'S VIEW OF CORE VALUE THERAPY

When I first learned about CVT and saw it demonstrated in participants during the workshop and observed their strong reactions, I remember thinking "This is so simple. This is so neat. This is it!"

The core value is at the heart of every personal problem, of every personal satisfaction and of every person. And it is as unique as the individual. It allows applying the lever at the root cause of distress or reoccurring conflict in someone's life, rather than addressing symptoms or modifying behaviour. CVT goes right to the core of an individual which influences their thoughts, feelings, behaviour and how they interpret interactions with the external world. Raising this core guiding rule of the individual's operating system to the surface brings a great sense of empowerment. I observed this in those who discover their core value for the first time: You can literally see them lift up, they can't hide from it, and they know it is true, because it is what defines them.

When I discovered my PCV, it was like I had been handed the weapon that had caused me pain, hurt and confusion (when I hurt others) all my life. All of a sudden I had this powerful tool in my hand, and rather than having it yielded against me, I am now able to use it for good towards others, but most importantly, have what validates me on tap.

Discovering and learning how to apply your PCV is a liberating and empowering experience as it puts you in charge of your interactions and responses to the external world and gives you unlimited access to having your value met by your sharing it with yourself and others.

I would like to add to this material from my experience, the PCV works both ways, in that it also highlights in the individual not only where there has been breach of their value, but also where they have been overdoing it. For example, if a person's PCV is 'acceptance', they may have felt hurt and disappointed in the past when others didn't interact with them in a way which made them feel accepted. Having had the PCV put into their control, they can now proactively act in accepting ways toward themselves and others. However, they may also discover as they look through their PCV lens, they have been accepting too much of what hasn't served them, e.g. blame from others or demand from others or that they have been accepting where they are in life, rather than challenging the status quo and making changes for the better etc.

Thus, discovering the PVC is discovering the 'key' to understanding oneself and enables the individual to assess and fine tune all aspects of their lives in accordance with it.

Beatrice McAlister (Student, Australian Institute of Professional Counsellors) 8th October 2018

CLIENT STORIES

CVT stories client have been de-identified

– Joe –

I first discovered core value therapy with a young man named Joe.

Joe was a handsome fella covered in some very nice ink, rather solid in build who was part of a motor bike club. He was a likeable fella with a warm rounded voice. He came for some anger management counselling. This alone was a major step for someone like him you may think and it probably was. He definitely fitted the alpha male profile.

At one point in the session Joe said "She presses my button, people press my buttons!"

I launched out of the chair and drew a button like shape

on the while board and said, "We are not leaving here until we discover what that button is."

That moment Core Value Therapy was birthed.

I asked Joe what made him angry to get a sense of his story. Someone dear to him had been unfaithful. This had made him very upset. When pressing him further, I enquired about other times he had been upset and he disclosed it was when people lied to him.

Again I asked him, "What bothers you about people lying to you?" I did this as you may to dig a little deeper in the real reason.

Joe replied, "I don't know, I hate people not telling me the Truth."

I didn't know then that the best way to help someone discover their core value was to have them reflect back and find the value word they used. At that time, I told Joe an individual's values are consistent and work through us all the times, and that he would sense when people are not being truthful. Joe replied, "Yes, that is the truth."

It is like a ship's radar sweeping around picking up the 'Truth' metre. I encouraged Joe to speak out the fact that he is picking up when people are lying to him and observe his reaction.

Joe said, "Won't this make me angrier?"

I said, "No, I don't think it will, you have to find another way of responding to the situation when you sense others are lying to you. You grill them about the circumstance to gather more information but that sends your 'Truth' alert button in high alert, because you are picking up further lies."

Joe said he would give it ago.

Joe returned to the next session and reported he could not believe the results. Someone had lied to him since we last spoke, and the first thing he observed about himself was that his emotions did not explode like they had before.

Joe said, "I looked at me stomach and was expecting it to explode and it didn't."

Joe went on to say he then out rightly told the person, he thought they 'were telling him a whopping Poky Pig.' Joe was still clam as he noticed the other persons looked caught out. Joe seem to enjoy that. This was quite a change to his previous reaction in such situations, when his anger would have been agitated. There was already an observable improvement regarding Joe's 'locus of control'.

At a further session I said to Joe, "What have you lied about?"

He said, "You are messing with me Dave, you are messing with me".

"No I am serious - For you to be so angry you must have lied about something", I said. Beneath the ice berg model are things like fear, values and beliefs.

Joe solemnly shared with me, "I have lied about being scared, scared of losing my girl."

I encourage Joe to go home and tell this to his partner. He did and when he returned reported, that his partner had never heard him be this honest and tell the truth about why he was really angry.

– Harry –

Harry was a slim young man in his mid-thirties and came to see me for counselling support because he had had two attempts on his life. Harry had such low self-esteem, he left a deep impression upon me. Harry had a very low demeanour, no confidence could be noted in his conversation and interaction in the session. Harry worked as a welder and for the past three years no one had talked to him. This sounded like an extreme example but he assured me that it was correct. The receptionist for the last three years had never acknowledged him, not one person had asked for help in a welding job. I assisted him to reveal his core value "acknowledge".

To break this down, I asked "How bad is wanting others to acknowledge you?"

He said, "Very bad, I want it all the time."

Part of core value therapy is to lower the need for the value to be fulfilled from others. I encouraged him to let it go using cognitive behaviour therapy and core value therapy.

I said, "When you go into work next, think to yourself 'I do not need to be acknowledged today.' Acknowledge for yourself, that you have worked to the best of your ability today."

Harry said, "I have got it".

It appeared he had indeed understood the concept. In the

following session, Harry came bounding into the room, a large smile beaming from ear to ear. He appeared to be very happy.

I asked Harry, "Are you on drugs Harry?"

He promptly replied, "No, I am not, but let me tell you what has happened. It took about two to three days and the first thing that occurred was, someone asked me to help them with their welding job. The next day the receptionist acknowledged me and said 'Good morning' to me. There is even have a girl interested in me now."

I said, "Stop it. Really all these things have happened?"

Harry said, "I want to write a book about the dramatic change that had occurred."

I said, "I would love to read it."

I scheduled another appointment and Harry maintained a 80% happiness result. Harrys self-esteem dramatically improved by lowering his need for others to acknowledge him and raise it within himself. The result is that he started receive the very thing he wanted, that is acknowledgement from others.

– John –

I saw John during a home visit through my private practise. John was a west coast miner. He was a large bearded well-built man with a reasonable amount of tattoos. His wife had initiated the session because of his anger. As we sat at the kitchen table, I asked him "What makes you angry?"

John went on to say he doesn't care anymore because people don't care about the things he lends them. Using Core Value therapy, I noticed he was saying "care" a lot.

I said, "John you appear to be a guy that would give your shirt off your back if someone needed it."

He said, "Yes I would"

I went on to say, "If someone's house was burning down you would get your truck and go and help them. Why because you..... care. "

John went on to tell me the main problem was when he lent his welder to someone, they returned it with wires exposed and when he went to use it later it could have killed him. This really made him mad. I linked the story to why he was angry because he cares for himself and someone had threatened that. John started to take this in. I mentioned to John, the important thing to remember that with a core value of "caring", he wants others to care for him and his things. Yet, he would also need to give the value away to others. Act in a caring way. This would be tested, but the answer is for him to give his 'care' value away.

At the next appointment John said he had been tested since we last spoke. The situation had been him coming home after a day mining. John had taken his work clothes off in the work shed next to the house at his wife's request. He is approached the backdoor of the house in nothing else but his 'jocks', in dark with freezing sleet falling.

John's wife met him at the back door, and said "Sorry dear, I forgot to get the wood, do you mind getting some?"

The wood was at least 50 metres away, stacked down the side of the property, in the weather, in the dark. John paused..... His thoughts started to race, "Doesn't she 'care' about me? I did what she wanted, I am half naked and she wants me to do more!"

He felt the anger boiling up in him as his value was being offended. But he also started to think, "Remembers give your value away, give your value away." Giving his value away would look like caring for his wife and do what she had asked. As quick as a whip John said "Sure, love." And off he went into the dark freezing cold night. He didn't just do one load he did several. John's wife's value is 'support' and she saw his actions as supporting her.

John reported to me over many months of communicating through email that he had never been angry again since that first discussion around his kitchen table and reveal to his family that his value was 'caring'. John's wife told him he is now continually caring for her and has improved as a father tremendously. Previously, the relationship was at rick of ending and John's engagement as a father was very low. He would come home from work and crack a beer and sit on the couch and watch TV. Now he comes home and asks what can he do to help his wife and engages with the boys in games and is involved with putting them to bed. I did not suggest any of these things. The correction of his value from 'you care for me' too 'I care for others' brought on this dramatic and ongoing change in his life.

There are many stories like these with clients but equally many more with professionals around this wonderful nation of ours who participate in the experiential nature of Core Value therapy training.

TESTIMONIALS

– Testimonials –

12 months ago our relationship was in a bad state, a number of different factors were causing us stress and instead of working together as a team we had started to resent each other. This is when we reached out and we were put in touch with David. Through working with David we learnt about the Love Languages and also discovered each of our core values. This was a very emotional and powerful journey for both of us. Trying to live by our core values has helped us immensely and our relationship is much stronger because of it. We still have our problems, we're only human but now we have the tools to deal with issues as they arise. We would recommend this form of counselling to others seeking help.

Marcus and Alannah

Thank you for the Core Values Training...I was doubtful at the beginning but actually experiencing your work was amazing. It was a very spiritual experience and has been transforming actually. It was a huge discovery and my self-esteem went up!!!! I am very grateful to you for facilitating this change.

Thank you, Turid

– Professional Training Feedback –

What impact will this training have on your work?

- *Give a new direction to use with some clients.*
- *Give extra insight and tools.*
- *Seeing much value in this approach in working with clients.*
- *Significant impact and keen to start practice incorporating CVT and learning more.*
- *A new way to have conversations with clients and create (hopefully) meaningful change in their lives.*
- *More understanding of values and how to talk with someone.*
- *Hopefully use it more in sessions with clients and incorporate into other therapies.*
- *Look into other ways of using some of what was learnt – feeling confident in doing so.*
- *Add to awareness working with clients/colleagues.*

- *Change the way I interact with clients and their issues.*
- *Listen to people in a different way.*
- *Another tool to help support clients.*
- *Helps to identify the values that drive clients and how they respond to situations.*
- *Be more mindful of values and how to help clients.*
- *Understanding how behaviour stems from the clients' core values.*
- *Reflect and build upon knowledge of personal own values and how they influence work/life.*
- *Identify personal core values which will assist to better work with and respect others.*

What topic/issue has been the most important for you?

- *Getting in tune with own core values and identifying them firstly.*
- *Listening and hearing own values.*
- *Understanding core values and learning to listen to observe this.*
- *Behaviour/functions stems from values.*
- *Identifying that I am not aware of what my core values are yet.*
- *Identifying how the core values are utilised i.e. from others, to ourselves, to others.*

- *Discovering my own value.*
- *Identifying core values – practice steps to achieve this*
- *Bringing it back to self.*
- *How to help someone find their core value.*
- *Listening intentionally to what clients are saying and hearing their values in that.*
- *Finding out what my personal core values are, those of other participants and breaking it down.*
- *Understanding we all have core values.*

Overall feedback

- *Excellent. Thank-you.*
- *Would have loved for it to be over 2 days to dig down more.*
- *I am excited to begin to try this new model. Thank-you.*

ACKNOWLEDGMENTS

I wish to acknowledge my wife firstly in the patience she has over the years listening to all the ideas I have and in helping me find my own core value. This is a core principal of CVT: You need others to help you discover it and that person was my wife. My greatest critic and greatest admirer. I love her greatly.

There are many professional people I wish to thank. Trevor Reeve, my former supervisor in the early years and now a dear friend. There were many hours spent discussing the model and designing a training package. You are truly a gracious and considerate human being who I am deeply fond of.

Sabrina Martin and Sinead Fahey Psychologist who have willingly spent countless hours in peer supervision over many years unlocking the depth of CVT especially some curly values, like the value of expectation! Thank you - you are both one of the best practitioners I have seen. Thank you for your wisdom advice and openly embracing CVT into your practise.

Larry Kalander former Area manager who walked with me in the earlier journey of Core Value therapy. Who asked me some amazing thoughtful questions that help me challenge and develop CVT.

Pastor Colin Brown who was with me through one of my most difficult times in my life, thank you.

Glenda Wadsley who offered her amazing editing skills which is clearly not my gift. Thanks Glenda for the many hours you have put in that has greatly helped the model be readable to a wider audience.

Beatrice McAlister who also kindly offered to format the publication. Bea your enthusiasm and quick adoption of CVT was truly impressive. You're a dynamo!

Robert Carrigan, manager of Australian Institute of Counselling Student centre Brisbane. Thank you for your encouragement and allowing me to come and teach AIPC students in CVT. A real honour and such a privilege to be able to do this. You are also an amazing man.

I wish to also thank Andrew King in supporting Core Value Therapy training throughout Australia. His continual encouragement to publish this book has eventually paid off.

To all the clients that have experienced CVT in their lives from the very first in January 2007 till now. You have shown and demonstrated the consistency of the results that CVT can achieve.

ABOUT THE AUTHOR

For the past 20 years, David has had a wide variety of counselling and professional experiences.

Author of 'What's for tea Dad'? and 'Honey I am Pregnant'.

As a counsellor, he has worked with people experiencing anger issues and conflict. From this work, David developed the Core Value Therapeutic model (CVT) in ©2007. This new therapy has greatly assisted many people in addressing anger management, emotional regulation, domestic violence, mental health issues and relationship breakdowns. David now travels throughout the nation training and presenting at conferences in CVT, Father Inclusive Practice, Mental Health in the workplace and Love Languages.

"I have a passion to help equip people to understand how they can improve their mental health so they can be emotionally healthy, live successfully and have lasting and fulfilling relationships." David Nancarrow

Ongoing training registrations can be located through:

Group Work Solutions National Training

www.groupworksolutions.com.au

CONFERENCES AND TRAINING

Core Value Conference Abstract Presentation Australia

2017 International Mental Health Conference: Brisbane
   CVT Abstract Published

2016 International Mental Health Conference: Brisbane
   CVT Abstract Published

2011 National Men and Family Relationship
   Conference: Newcastle University Abstract Published

2010 Disability Conference: Hobart

2009 MFR Conference Western Australia Abstract Published

www.ingramcontent.com/pod-product-compliance
Lightning Source LLC
Chambersburg PA
CBHW021838020426
42334CB00014B/687